THE BRITISH MUSEUM

HINDU

VISIONS OF THE SACRED

ஸ்ரீ சார்ங்கபாணி ஸ்வாமி கோவில்
SRI SARANGAPANI SWAMI TEMPLE

THE BRITISH MUSEUM

HINDU

VISIONS OF THE SACRED

A.L. Dallapiccola

THE BRITISH MUSEUM PRESS

The author is grateful to Mr T.R. Blurton of the British Museum Department of
Asia for his valuable suggestions and continuous encouragement.

Photography by The British Museum Department of Photography and Imaging,
C. Branfoot and A.L. Dallapiccola

A catalogue record for this book is available from the British Library

ISBN 0 7141 2432-0

Frontispiece: The eastern gateway of the Sarangapani Swami Temple,
Kumbakonam, Tamil Nadu.

Designed and typeset in Centaur by Peter Ward
Printed in China by C&C Offset

CONTENTS

Kolams, auspicious drawings made with coloured powder or rice flour, are drawn afresh each day before sunrise at the threshold of the home by the women of the house

INTRODUCTION

D ESPITE THE differences in language, culture, religious tradition, dress and diet that exist among the diverse groups that form the population of India, the cohesive force which unites the Hindu majority are a number of shared values which constitute Hinduism.

Contemporary Hinduism is a complex religious system. It encompasses different cults which are focused around various gods, principally Shiva, Vishnu and the great goddess Devi, or Shakti. There are many diverse schools of thought, many gods and goddesses, ascetics, deified heroes and semi-divine beings, each with their own rich and occasionally chaotic mythologies.

It would therefore be wiser to speak about Hinduisms, each linked by various common elements such as Vedic tradition, the caste system, religious and moral law, epics and myths, and reverence for spiritual teachers.

The basis of Hindu belief rests in the four *Vedas* (the oldest of which dates from *c.* 1500-1200 BC). These are sacred texts in Sanskrit, thought to be composed by the Aryans. These collections of hymns celebrate deities and mention many of the gods which are still worshipped in Hindu belief even today. The Vedic religion (also known as Brahmanism) centres upon rituals of sacrifice performed only by Brahmin priests. The gods are reinvigorated through sacrifice and in turn ensure the well-being of mankind.

A striking feature of Hinduism is that it has no unique doctrinal basis apart from acknowledging the authority of the Vedic tradition. In the last two thousand years or so all these religious traditions co-existed, although not always peacefully: dissent and heterodoxy created new schools of thought.

In Hindu thought time is cyclical, one era follows another until the time of destruction comes and, after a period of quiescence, creation starts afresh. This alternating rhythm of creation and destruction is related to the concept of light and darkness. The unresolved, continuous tension between positive and negative forces, the main theme of Hindu mythology, is expressed in the everlasting conflicts between the gods and their rivals, the anti-gods (*asuras*).

Traditional Hindu society is divided into four main castes: the Brahmins, the warriors, the agriculturalists and traders, and the menials. The Brahmins' privilege and duty is to study the sacred literature and to perform ceremonies on behalf of the rest of society. Each individual is expected to obey and fulfil his or her obligation to society which varies according to one's sex, stage in life, and the caste into which one is born. This belief is connected to the notion of rebirth. Every person is seen as part of the continuous cycle of rebirth and one's present position in society is determined by how well the duties of a previous life have been carried out. It is the wish to break this cycle of death and rebirth which is the preoccupation of not only Hinduism, but also Jainism and Buddhism.

The basis of Hindu philosophical thought is contained in a group of about thirteen texts, the *Upanishads*, composed between *c.* 700 and 300 BC and subsequently revised at various times. Their teachings focus on the following points: the essential identity of *brahman*, the divine source of the universe, and that of *atman* or the innermost self of man. As long as man is unaware of this identity he is subject to an endless series of rebirths according to his *karma*, one's good or bad actions. When he realizes the identity of *brahman* and *atman* he will find the way to attain spiritual liberation, but to gain this insight he must discard all worldly concerns and embark on a path of meditation and discipline.

Hinduism has often been described in western literature as mystical and spiritual, and Hindu culture as other-worldly. But this claim fades away when one is confronted with the sensuous experience of Hindu religious practice. Day to day worship is based not on abstract truths written in the texts but on the concrete representation of the divine. Worship involves all the senses: one sees the image, touches it, hears the sound of the bells and the prayers, smells the burning incense, and eats the consecrated food.

The Indian term for knowing is *darshana* which means 'seeing' and this speaks volumes about the crucial role of vision in Hindu religion. Seeing is the central act of worship for a Hindu because communication between the human and the divine is established through the eyes. The worshipper beholds the image of a god and, simultaneously, is seen by it.

Therefore, the need to give a form to the divine (*murti*) is the main source of inspiration behind most of India's visual arts. The sustained and consistent preoccupation with the rendering of an essentially unknown entity has resulted in a remarkable array of sacred images which are linked to Hindu myth. They range from crude terracotta figurines, which are worshipped in rural settings, to exquisite icons in stone and bronze enshrined in temples. Never intended to be displayed as works of art in museums, they are created by believers to portray the spiritual.

Hinduism was 'exported' overseas in the nineteenth century. Renowned spiritual personalities spread its message among non-Hindus, while Hindu expatriate communities built temples in their new surroundings. Its ability to develop, evolve and incorporate the new indicates why it remains such a relevant belief system to over a fifth of the world's population. It is a positive, dynamic, all-embracing way of life with each believer having a particular place and role in Hindu order.

Sacred knowledge

VEDIC LITERATURE

THE MOST IMPORTANT scriptures of Hinduism are the *Vedas* 'knowledge'. Composed in an ancient form of Sanskrit and believed to be of supernatural origin, they were apparently revealed to the sages of old by the god Brahma. The *Vedas* and their teachings are believed to be eternal and infallible, and form the basis of Hindu religion and ethics.

The *Vedas* mainly consist of four collections of hymns, detached verses and sacrificial formulas. The earliest and foremost of the four collections is the *Rig Veda* 'Veda of Praise' which was probably composed between 1500 and 1200 BC. It contains hymns to the main Aryan deities such as Surya, Agni, Indra and others. For a long time these hymns, which are still an integral part of Hindu ritual, were transmitted orally from generation to generation.

Besides the four Vedas are a number of other sacred works: the *Brahmanas* are manuals for the correct performance of rituals, the *Aranyakas* an appendix to the *Brahmanas*, and the concluding part of Vedic literature are the *Upanishads*, a series of philosophical and mystical texts.

Vedic knowledge is taught in special schools where Brahmin boys spend some twelve years memorizing hundreds of verses and acquiring the necessary skills to correctly perform various rituals.

South Indian guru and disciples. The three horizontal white marks on
their foreheads and bodies show them to be followers of the god Shiva, *c.* 1925

EPIC LITERATURE

WHILE VEDIC LITERATURE, 'revealed' by Brahma, is accessible only to the twice-born (the first three castes of Indian society) the teachings contained in the epics, the *Puranas*, and other mythological works are shared by the whole population.

The *Ramayana* 'Rama's career' is one of two great Indian epics. Its presumed author is the sage Valmiki. The poem was probably composed between the 4th century BC and the 3rd century AD. In due course the original Sanskrit text was elaborated upon in the regional languages and embellished with local myths. The adventures of Rama, his wife Sita and his brother Lakshmana culminate in Sita's abduction by Ravana, the king of Lanka and, eventually, in her rescue at the hands of Rama and his allies. The tales are very popular not only in India but throughout Asia and their impact on culture and art cannot be overstated.

The other great Sanskrit epic is the *Mahabharata* 'the great *bharata*' possibly the longest poem in the world. This work, probably compiled between the 3rd century BC and the 4th century AD, is attributed to the mythical sage, Vyasa. The core of the poem describes the contest between two related families, the Kauravas and the Pandavas, for the conquest of Bharata or Upper India. The year-long strife culminates in a fierce war from which the five Pandava heroes emerge victorious. Eventually they renounce their kingdom, retire to the Himalayas, and ascend to Indra's heaven. A substantial number of myths, theological and ethical teachings, folk tales and philosophical passages were incorporated into the original story. Furthermore, a vast number of poets and editors representing different schools of thought have tampered with the original text so that different philosophical views appear in the poem.

Rama, on the shoulders of the monkey-hero Hanuman, kills Ravana,
painting on paper, Thanjavur or Tiruchirappalli, *c.* 1820

PURANAS

THE *Puranas* 'old stories' are collections of ancient myths concerning a variety of topics. These range from the creation of the universe, its destruction and re-creation, to the genealogies of various gods and the history of mythical dynasties. The narratives are interspersed with a wealth of information on theology, philosophy, science, ritual, astrology, architecture and iconography, and much more. The works, written in Sanskrit, are couched in a dialogue between the main narrator — generally a sage — and his disciples, whose questions anticipate those of the actual listeners. Through the *Puranas* the principles of religion and ethics are disseminated among women, the illiterate, and all others who are prohibited from access to Vedic tradition. There are eighteen major and eighteen minor *Puranas*. The oldest of these narratives was composed in about the 6th century AD. Among the most important *Puranas* is the *Bhagavata Purana* (*c.* 9th-10th century) which centres upon Krishna's life and career in great detail. A pivotal text for understanding the Krishna cult, this work is one of the most popular of the *Puranas*, often recited and commented upon in public.

The Puranic tradition continues, albeit on a less ambitious scale. Nowadays, *Puranas* celebrating a local deity or a sacred site are written for the benefit of visitors in both English and one of the regional languages.

Krishna steals the clothes of the milkmaids,
ivory plaque, south India, 17th-18th century

Hindu Society

CASTES

THE EARLIEST ACCOUNT of Hindu social structure is found in a hymn from the *Rig Veda*. According to this the four castes originate from the dismembered body of the cosmic man, the source of all creation.

Society is divided into four occupational categories each corresponding to a particular limb of the cosmic man. From his mouth came the Brahmins, the priestly class; from his arms emerged the *kshatriyas* or warrior class; from his thighs the *vaishyas*, the commercial class and from his feet the *shudras*, both artisans and menials.

The first three classes are known as 'twice-born' because, metaphorically speaking, they are reborn when they are invested with the sacred thread, a ceremony which boys undergo between the age of eight and twelve. The first three castes – especially the Brahmins – are allowed access to the 'revealed knowledge'. The fourth class comprising the *shudras* and a sizeable quantity of *Dalits* 'oppressed', formerly called outcastes and including India's large tribal population, are not allowed to undergo the sacred thread ceremony. They are barred from studying the sacred texts and were excluded from entering temples until the Temple Act of 1948.

The complex social structure of India fascinated the British during the colonial period who commissioned sets of paintings showing the various castes and trades.

A potter at work while his wife sells clay images.
This painting is likely to be one of a set illustrating the various castes
and trades, probably by Siva Dayal Lal, Patna, *c.* 1870

ASCETICISM

HINDU PHILOSOPHY views reality as a temporary illusion, as if conjured up by magic. Mankind lives under the illusion of being in control whereas, in fact, everything is determined by *maya*, the power of delusion which creates, destroys and re-creates everything. All people under the thrall of *maya* are endlessly subject to the cycle of death and rebirth whereas those who realize the illusory nature of reality will strive for spiritual freedom and thereby avoid rebirth. One of the ways to spiritual freedom is through meditation, penance and asceticism.

Indian culture has created a whole mythology around ascetics and seers who seek spiritual emancipation. They play a major role in the epics, *Puranas* and folklore. Described as extraordinary characters who renounce the world, they live in the wilderness and undergo the most excruciating penances to attain spiritual freedom, supernatural wisdom and magical powers. While being great teachers, poets and philosophers, they can be notoriously difficult. If accidentally disturbed while meditating or inadvertently offended their anger can unleash cataclysmic disasters, threatening not only mankind but also the supremacy of the gods.

Asceticism is not only practised to acquire spiritual merits. It can be a means to force the gods to grant favours as shown in the many myths in which an anti-god (*asura*) undergoes extreme penance in attempt to gain favours. In the long run, these prove to be fatal because the gods always manage to overcome the anti-gods.

Rama, Sita and Lakshmana visiting a group of ascetics in the wilderness,
detail from a painted cloth depicting the *Ramayana*, Tamil Nadu
or Sri Lanka, 19th century

MEMORIALS

Sati and hero stones

THE TERM *sati* means 'true, good and virtuous'. It is applied to women who, on their husband's death, either threw themselves on his pyre or committed suicide shortly afterwards. This act expresses the unbreakable bond between husband and wife and is believed to increase the family's merit and honour. A *sati* is regarded as a goddess and becomes a manifestation of the goddess Sati, Shiva's wife, who also proved her worthiness to her husband. A *sati's* sacrifice is commemorated by a specially carved stone slab which either depicts her with her husband or simply shows her right arm decorated with bangles to symbolize married status. It is bent at the elbow with an extended palm, blessing family and relatives.

Another type of memorial, fairly widespread throughout India, is the hero stone. Like the *sati* stone it is a carved slab which commemorates an act of valour that resulted in the hero's death: an act of gallantry in war, recovering stolen cattle, protecting the honour of women, killing wild animals or death in shipwreck. Generally, three scenes are carved onto the slab. The bottom panel shows the circumstances of the hero's death; the central panel depicts his ascent to heaven in a temple-like conveyance flanked by heavenly nymphs and other celestial beings; in the top panel he is seen worshipping a *linga*, the symbol of the god Shiva.

Sati stone, Kaikini, Uttara Kannada district, Karnataka,
probably end of the 14th or beginning of the 15th century

HINDU DIASPORA

In the nineteenth century a number of Chettiars, a prosperous banking community from Tamil Nadu, migrated to other parts of the British Empire, especially Burma, Malaysia and Mauritius. Once successfully established they kept in contact with their native towns and part of their profits were sent to support religious and social institutions.

At the beginning of the twentieth century, artisans and traders mainly from Gujarat and Punjab migrated to east Africa, some employed by the British administration and others to set up their own businesses. Gradually, they promoted social and educational institutions and generously supported religious activities. They, too, kept in close touch with India. The situation was different for those who were hired by the British and the Dutch in the mid-nineteenth century and transported to Trinidad, Guyana and Surinam. When their contracts expired only a minority decided to return to India. Most acquired land and settled in their new surroundings, still clinging, however, to their Hindu traditions.

After World War II, in the wake of political changes – especially in east Africa during the 1960s and '70s – a great number of Indians migrated to Britain. Later, a new wave of highly qualified and skilled professionals left India and established themselves in Malaysia, Australia, the USA and Canada. Despite the totally alien environment Hindu communities thrived: impressive temples were built, Brahmin priests came from India and traditional religious practices gained a new momentum.

Swaminarayan Temple, Neasden, London, built in 1995

Worship

TEMPLE

A TEMPLE is not only the house of a god but, more significantly, where the divine and human worlds meet. The temple's most important feature is the sanctuary, a small dark room where the symbol or the image of the god is enshrined. These images are placed at the intersection of the horizontal and vertical axes of the building so that their power radiates both outwards through the walls and upwards. Above the sanctuary rises a tower. On its summit, aligned with the image, is a pot-shape which represents the vessel containing the nectar of immortality, source of everlasting revival. The tip of the pot marks the intersection between the worlds of the gods and that of mankind.

The vessel with the nectar of immortality refers to a myth in which the gods see creation withering away and decide to revive it. To do this they must retrieve the vessel with the nectar of immortality which is stored in the depths of the Ocean of Milk. The Ocean has to be churned and so the gods enlist the help of their rivals, the *asuras*, promising them a share of the nectar. Needless to say, the gods keep the nectar to themselves, drink their fill and once reinvigorated defeat their rivals. The pot thereby became a symbol of both creation and renewal.

Devotees walk clockwise around the building paying homage to the deities set in the building's niches while looking at the carvings adorning its walls. On entering the temple they progress through pillared halls to the dim interior and reach the main sanctuary where they can view the image, thereby making a direct link with the deity through eye contact.

Bhutanatha temple, Badami, Karnataka, 7th-11th century

DEVOTEE AT WORSHIP

ONE OF THE most revered of Vishnu's manifestations is Venkateshvara or Balaji whose temple is picturesquely sited on Tirumala hill, a short distance from the bustling town of Tirupati in Andhra Pradesh. The Tirumala-Venkateshvara temple — believed to be the richest of the whole of India and second only to the Vatican — is visited daily by some 25,000 visitors. Because of the crowds it is not possible to look at the figure of Venkateshvara at leisure, but the lasting impression is of a form swathed in silk garments, covered in floral wreaths and opulent jewels, bright in a dark, constricted and stifling setting.

In his upper hands the god carries the discus (symbol of the sun) and a conch (symbol of space). The lower right hand is in the wish-fulfilling posture and the left rests on the thigh. A golden sword hangs from his belt.

This painting shows, with documentary precision, the 'flower ritual' which is celebrated every Thursday evening in the Venkateshvara temple. On this occasion the image is completely clad with flowers. A devotee, possibly the individual who offered the floral decoration, is depicted respectfully paying homage to the god.

A devotee at worship, painting on paper, possibly from Srirangapatna, early 18th century

IMAGES CARRIED IN PROCESSION

THE TEMPLES' metal images are periodically carried outside on palanquins, accompanied by a procession of devotees holding standards, umbrellas, fans and torches. Generally, those who carry the palanquins are selected from special families who have been entrusted with this honour for generations. The procession stops at houses of devotees who offer gifts and refreshments to those who carry the palanquins and their followers. This gives the crowds the opportunity of coming as near to the images as possible, to touch the palanquins, and to receive some of the flowers or leaves decorating the images.

On the first palanquin is Ganesha, one of the two sons of Shiva, standing propped up by a huge bolster. Ganesha 'Lord of the Beginnings' is always invoked before any new undertaking, the first to be worshipped in a ritual and at the head of every procession.

On the second is Subrahmanya, Shiva's second son, and his son's two consorts. On the third are Shiva and Parvati in their Himalayan home, Mount Kailasha, and imprisoned beneath the mountain is the ten-headed Ravana, king of Lanka. The tableau illustrates a well-known mythological incident. Ravana flew in his aerial chariot towards the Himalayas but, on entering the aerial space above Mount Kailasha, he was prevented by one of Shiva's attendants. At this, the incensed Ravana tried to uproot Mount Kailasha. The mountain swayed and swerved and Parvati, in a fright, clung to Shiva who, with a movement of his toe, stabilized the mountain which imprisoned Ravana beneath it. For thousands of years Ravana sung the praises of Shiva until he was forgiven and gifted with a divine sword. Almost two centuries have passed, yet today's processions look remarkably similar to the one illustrated here.

Images carried in procession, pen and ink drawing on European paper,
Tiruchirappalli or perhaps Thanjavur, *c.* 1820

PROCESSIONAL CHARIOTS

METAL IMAGES are not only paraded on palanquins but also in beautifully carved chariots. The chariot festival is one of the main events in the religious calendar of a temple and a key attraction for devotees who come in droves to witness the event. The sumptuously decorated images (*murtis*) are taken from the sanctuary and placed on the chariots which are then pulled around the temple and along the traditional processional road by devotees specially chosen for the task. The road either skirts the peripheral walls of the temple or leads to the temple pool. The crowds try to touch the chariot, wishing to be sanctified by the image, but usually have to be content with reverently touching the ropes which pull it.

The chariot is a simple chassis made of solid wood, with wooden wheels whose rim is reinforced with metal. Numerous carvings of incidents from Hindu mythology adorn its sides. On festive days, a tower-like structure of bamboo and matting is mounted on the chassis and then decorated with coloured cloths, tinsel, garlands, and ornaments such as papier mâché figures of horses and winged creatures. After special ceremonies the image is placed on the chariot. Priests stand nearby and fan it with fans or fly-whisks, collect gifts from the crowds of mainly flowers or food which are offered first to the image, blessed by it, and then distributed as *prasada* (favour) among the devotees.

After the images have been out of the sacred temple precincts they need to be cleansed of all impurities with which they have had contact. This is done with special ceremonies and then the images are returned to their shrines.

Processional chariot, Shantadurga Temple, Fatorpa, Goa

VOWS

Vows play an important role in Hindu religious life. Individuals undergo special vows such as fasting on specific days, visiting a particular temple, reciting special prayers and undertaking pilgrimages in order to fulfil an obligation towards a deity. Some pilgrims choose to perform their journey on foot, prostrating themselves, rolling on the ground or hopping on one foot, to mention just a few. The more difficult the progress the more merit is gained. Vows are taken either to obtain a favour from a god or by way of thanksgiving.

The carving shows the penance which Arjuna undertook to obtain from Shiva a miraculous weapon which would enable him to conquer his enemies. This story is one of the most famous of the great epic the *Mahabharata*.

Arjuna, one of the five Pandava princes, retreated to the forest where he engaged in severe penance. Dressed in bark clothes, with unkempt hair, he ate only every few days and eventually reduced his intake of food until he lived solely on air. For years he stood motionless on one foot until one day Shiva and Parvati, dressed as mountain dwellers, chanced in that part of the forest for a hunting spree. At that very moment a huge boar appeared and prepared to attack Arjuna but both the hero and Shiva were quick to shoot their arrows and kill it. A violent discussion ensued between Arjuna and Shiva as to who had killed the boar. This was followed by a tremendous fight which Arjuna eventually lost. Such was his prowess, however, that Shiva granted his wish and handed him the magical weapon.

Shiva grants the magical weapon to Arjuna, detail from a rock carving depicting Arjuna's penance, Mamallapuram, Tamil Nadu, 7th century

PILGRIMAGE

INDIA IS RICH in holy places (*tirthas*). Often set in dramatic surroundings they are connected with a specific god or mythical event. Visiting them is one of the important religious duties of a Hindu. A pilgrimage is not only considered to please the relevant god but to also give inner peace and increase the devotee's merit.

Particularly commendable are visits to the seven holy cities: Ayodhya, Mathura, Gaya, Varanasi, Ujjain, Hardwar and Dwarka, and the four 'abodes of light' sited at the four cardinal points of the subcontinent: Badrinath in the north, Puri in the east, Rameshvaram in the south and Dwarka in the west.

It is, however, Varanasi which is the holiest of the holy cities of India, situated on the sacred river Ganges. Known for a long time as Banaras or Benares, it reverted to its original name of Varanasi in 1947. According to Hindu tradition Varanasi contains the whole world, everything that is good and holy on earth, all the sacred sites and sacred rivers of India, and all the gods. Dying in Varanasi liberates one from the never-ending pilgrimage through many lives. It is here that all sins are washed away in the waters of the Ganges.

Some sacred sites, especially in south India, are connected either with manifestations of the same deity (such as the nine aspects of Vishnu worshipped in nine different places along the Tambraparni river) or with events in the career of one single god such as the six sites sacred to the god Subrahmanya, one of Shiva's sons.

This plan of Puri, the most important pilgrimage town on the Bay

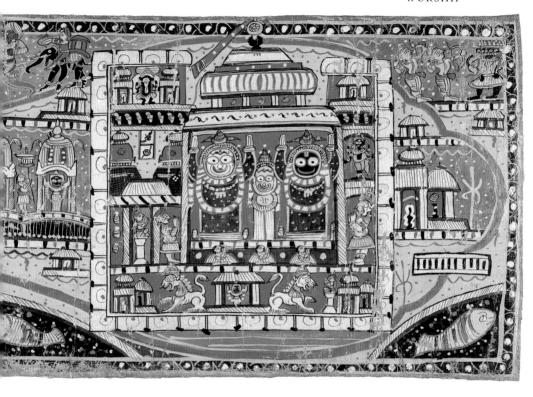

Plan of Puri, painting on cloth, Orissa, late 19th century

of Bengal, shows the main temple enshrining the city's three main gods: Jagannath, an aspect of Krishna (right), his brother Balabhadra (left) and their sister Subhadra (centre). The central sanctuary, surrounded by smaller buildings, is enclosed by a wall. Three ceremonial chariots of the divine trio are shown on the left. The plan of the town is conch-shaped because it is believed that Puri represents Vishnu's conch.

MAKAMAKAM FESTIVAL

SOME FESTIVALS are celebrated every few years. Their date depends on complicated calculations involving the position of the planets, specific stars and the full moon. For instance, the great Kumbhamela festival is celebrated in the northern city of Prayaga (formerly known as Allahabad) every twelve years when the sun enters Aries and Jupiter is in Aquarius.

In southern India the Makamakam festival at Kumbakonam in Tamil Nadu is celebrated every eleven or twelve years when Jupiter enters the constellation of Leo at the full moon of the Tamil month of *Thai* (February-March). Crowds of pilgrims visit the town to wade through the shallow waters of the Makamakam pool, one of the most sacred landmarks of the site. They sprinkle themselves with the water of various springs that feed it – a ritual which is believed to cleanse one from every sin. The event lasts nine days. On this occasion, the metal images from the many temples of the town are paraded on palanquins or chariots along the streets of the town.

This picture was taken on the ninth and last day of the Makamakam festival, February 18, 1992. To the right is a huge cut-out image of the Chief Minister of Tamil Nadu, Dr (Ms) Jayalalitha, who was among the pilgrims on that occasion.

The final day of Makamakam festival, Kumbakonam, 1992

CALENDAR PRINTS

PILGRIMS TEND TO travel lightly with a bundle of clothes in a shoulder bag and a water flask. Temples, religious and charitable institutions provide them with food and shelter. It is usual to buy mementoes of a visit to a holy place and the past decades have witnessed the rapid development of a whole industry of religious souvenirs ranging from prints to three-dimensional images.

In bygone days visitors bought paintings on paper and cloth. These showed the main god enshrined and surrounded by the lesser gods and goddesses in their temples. The salient landmarks of the site and the legend connected to it were also depicted. Vibrant prints have now superseded these but, as in the past, once the pilgrims return home the picture will be framed, hung on a wall with other images of gods, and cherished as a memento of their pilgrimage.

By the beginning of the twentieth century, paintings on paper and cloth were replaced by mass-produced, vividly coloured prints. It is not known exactly when this type of popular art was introduced to India but the first prints showing Indian gods and goddesses were produced in southern Germany by presses which specialized in Roman Catholic devotional material. This extremely successful genre developed according to the aesthetics of regional Indian styles but during the last thirty years or so it has been strongly influenced by the film industry. The faces of the gods and goddesses copy those of the leading film stars of the moment and their costumes are based on those seen in mythological films.

On the hill summit of Pavagadh (Gujarat) is an important shrine dedicated to the goddess Bhavani. The print shows the way to the temple and other sacred landmarks which pilgrims should visit en route.

The route to Pavagadh, coloured print on paper, India, *c.* 1973

SNAKE-DEITIES

Snake worship has a long history in India. The snakes (*nagas*) are a category of powerful semi-divine beings. These half-human and half-snake beings are thought to be the guardians of gems and precious minerals. Famous for their wisdom, skill, supernatural powers and beauty, they play a major role in folklore and in Hindu, Buddhist and Jaina mythology.

Traditionally, they have been associated with fertility, water – especially pools and rivers where they are reputed to dwell – and with tree worship. With their capacity to slough their skin, snakes are also a symbol of immortality and the ever-revolving cycle of time.

A common sight throughout south India are votive slabs bearing the effigy of a snake near a well or beneath a sacred tree. These are set up by women desiring children. An open-air shrine for the snakes is a feature of every south Indian temple.

Snake stones in Malpe, Udupi district, Karnataka

SACRED TREES

Tree spirits and trees, especially old and large ones, play a major role in Indian folklore and mythology. Associated with spiritual powers, trees sheltered many mythical and religious personalities steeped in meditation. The Buddha, for instance, attained enlightenment beneath a tree. A number of Hindu deities are associated with a specific tree which, growing in the temple precincts, is the object of special worship.

Tree worship is very popular in rural areas. A common sight are trees with trunks draped in sarees, its branches decorated with long strips of cloth. Miniature cradles, green glass bangles and other ornaments hang among the foliage. Occasionally, a small shrine dedicated to a local goddess is located nearby.

Cradles and lengths of cloth hanging from the branch of a sacred tree near the
shrine of the goddess Esakki Amman, Tirunelveli district, Tamil Nadu

RURAL SHRINES

A substantial number of village deities, mainly goddesses, are worshipped in rural areas. Village goddesses are closely associated with the cycle of seasons and agricultural activities. They are the source of life and prosperity for the community. Highly temperamental, they have to be pacified with blood sacrifices and alcohol libations to avoid famine, drought, epidemics and other natural calamities.

Their images, occasionally highly stylized, are fashioned in clay or other fragile materials and are located in open-air shrines in fields, groves and remote locations. Occasionally, they share their name with some important classical goddess but their appearance and their cycle of myths are very different.

A few male deities appear in the entourage of the goddesses. One of the most prominent in Tamil Nadu is Aiyanar, a benevolent deity and the watchman of the village who patrols the area on his horse at night.

Open-air shrine with Aiyanar's clay steeds, spears stuck in the ground and images
of the goddesses beneath the tree, Coimbatore district, Tamil Nadu

Shiva

LINGA

SHIVA, whose name means 'auspicious', is the most paradoxical among the Hindu gods because of his many contrasting aspects. Shiva is an ascetic but also the husband of Parvati, a householder, a musician and dancer, the creator and destroyer of all things, and both male and female being. He lives at the edges of civilization near burning grounds accompanied by his attendants the elephants (*ganas*).

The main image enshrined in the sanctuary of Shaiva temples is that of Shiva as a *linga* 'sign, gender, phallus'. Placed at the centre of the building it radiates energy. The *linga* is the symbol which represents Shiva as the male principle and the energy which underlies creation. Every creation cycle emanates from the *linga* and, at the end of each cycle, creation is re-absorbed into it.

A *linga* is a vertical stone shaft with a rounded top which emerges from a circular base. The base represents the female generative organ '*yoni*'. A spout placed at the side of the *yoni* serves as a drain through which the water and other offerings poured onto the *linga* flow away.

The *linga* and the *yoni* represent the union of Shiva and Shakti (power) and ultimately, the union of male and female powers.

Linga decorated with hibiscus flowers in the courtyard of Someshvara Temple, Barkur, Karnataka, 16th century

LINGODBHAVAMURTI – SHIVA EMERGES FROM THE LINGA

THIS POWERFUL IMAGE of Shiva emerging from the fiery *linga* combines the symbol of Shiva with an actual depiction of the god.

The story behind this image is one of the most famous in Hindu mythology. While the gods Brahma and Vishnu were arguing over who was the more powerful between them they saw a huge pillar of fire, the *linga*, arising from the waters of the ocean. Anxious to discover where the *linga* originated and ended they assumed animal forms. Brahma as a gander flew upwards, Vishnu as a boar dived into the water. Both failed to fathom the *linga* of fire. Brahma, however, seeing a flower floating through the air caught it and claimed to have reached the top of the *linga*, a lie that was to cost him his head. While in discussion, the blazing *linga* split open and Shiva appeared before the two gods who respectfully paid homage to him. Thus, Shiva established his supremacy and subsequently the *linga* was worshipped on earth as his symbol.

The climax of the story is shown opposite: the four-armed figure of Shiva emerges surrounded by a mandorla of flames from the pillar-like *linga*. The gander is depicted at the top of the *linga* and the boar burrowing the earth at the bottom.

Shiva emerging from the *linga*, carving in stone, Kampahareshvara Temple, Tribhuvanam, Tamil Nadu, late 12th century

TRIDENT

THE TRIDENT is one of the usual attributes with which Shiva is shown. As is the case with the weapons brandished by different gods, the trident not only signifies the destruction of evil but also the bestowal of grace because it severs the human soul from the endless cycle of reincarnation. Thus, the trident becomes an object of devotion explaining why such images are produced and regularly worshipped.

This remarkable bronze shows the god Shiva leaning elegantly against his conveyance, the bull Nandi, who symbolizes the god's virility and strength. The features of the image as well as the details of the clothes and jewellery have been obliterated by a millennium of ritual lustrations and from being touched by devotees. The god and Nandi emerge from the central prong of the trident and are surrounded by the external prongs whose elegant, curved shape lends a frame. The epiphany of the god and his bull from the upright prong is reminiscent of the emergence of Shiva from the fiery pillar. This work expresses beautifully the essential identity between Shiva, the bull Nandi and the trident.

Trident with Shiva as rider of the bull, bronze, Tamil Nadu, *c.* 950

BHAIRAVA – THE TERRIBLE OR FRIGHTFUL

HINDU GODS have complex and often paradoxical personalities. Each has a positive and a negative side. In order to express these different character traits the same deity is represented in many different forms, each with a specific name. The different characters of each god are significant because each reflects a facet of life. Shiva, whose name means 'auspicious', is a good example. He is the creator and destroyer of the universe, both male and female, a great ascetic but also a family-man, and many more besides.

While the *linga* expresses Shiva's creative power, Bhairava 'terrible' personifies Shiva's wrath and his darkest side. The representations of Bhairava, such as the one opposite, stress dramatically his awesome aspect. He is depicted naked except for his ornaments and a garland of skulls draped around his body. His matted hair and high sandals are typical of wandering beggars. Round, bulging eyes and protruding fangs emphasize his violent nature. In the upper pair of hands are the two typical attributes of Shiva, the trident and the hourglass-shaped drum around which a cobra is coiled. In the lower left hand is a severed head and a skull cup. The lower right, now empty, would have probably carried a sword. Bhairava is followed by a dog – the most impure of animals – licking the blood which oozes from the severed head.

Bhairava, bronze, Karnataka, *c.* 950

GANGADHARAMURTI – SHIVA AS CARRIER OF THE RIVER GANGES

RIVERS AND POOLS are worshipped as givers of life and sustainers of the community. Although almost any expanse of water is sacred there are seven rivers which are imbued with special sanctity: Ganga, Yamuna, Sarasvati, Godavari, Narmada and Kaveri. The Ganges (Ganga) and her tributary the Jumna (Yamuna) are two of the most important. They are visualized as goddesses and their voluptuous images grace the entrance to all sacred precincts. Their auspicious presence purifies the visitors before entering the temple complex.

According to myth, the Ganga – the most sacred of all Indian rivers – used to flow through the heavens. In order to bring her to earth to purify the ashes of his ancestors and enable them to ascend to heaven, King Bhagiratha practised severe austerities. His penance pleased Shiva and the river was allowed to descend to earth. The god graciously intercepted the tremendous impact of the cascading river with his head and saved the earth from being devastated by its force. After roaming among the matted locks of Shiva the Ganges found its way to earth and to the netherworld where the ashes of Bhagiratha's ancestors were purified by her waters.

Shiva as Gangadhara, calendar for the year 1914 with coloured print based on a painting by R. Ravi Varma (1848-1906)

NATARAJA – THE LORD OF THE DANCE

IN RECENT CENTURIES this image of Shiva Nataraja or Shiva as 'Lord of the Dance' has become one of the most famous of Hindu India. The icon was created over a thousand years ago in south India.

The figure is placed on a pedestal from which issues a halo of flames. In his upper right hand the god carries an hourglass-shaped drum, in the left, a blazing flame. The lower hands are free of emblems, the right points to the sky and the other to the deformed creature who represents ignorance, crushed beneath his foot. The conspicuous crescent moon on the side of his head symbolizes time. The differently shaped earrings reveal the androgynous nature of the god.

The image of Shiva as Nataraja is a visual rendering of the five cosmic activities of a god: creation arises from the drum's sound; protection comes from the raised hand; destruction proceeds from the fire; the raised foot gives salvation and the foot firmly planted on the dwarfish creature gives refuge to the soul enmeshed in the toils of human life.

Shiva Nataraja, bronze, Tamil Nadu, 10th century

THE FAMILY OF SHIVA

SHIVA IS ALSO, albeit reluctantly, a family-man. The story of his marriage to Parvati narrates how the great god was distracted from his meditation for a split second by arrows fired at him by the god of love. In that fateful moment he noticed the beauty of Parvati who stood before him. A staunch devotee of Shiva, she had set her heart upon marrying him since her childhood. She engaged in a long period of severe austerities during which she existed only on air, stood in water during the winter, and during the summer sat motionless beneath the sun, surrounded by four fires. She was visited by various sages who tested her steadfastness. Although her answers satisfied them, Shiva was not fully convinced by Parvati's devotion and appeared before her in disguise asking her some difficult theological questions. Eventually, he revealed his true identity and Parvati became his wife. They did not live 'happily ever after' and their union was punctuated by conflicts such as Parvati's jealousy of her own sister, Ganga, who nestled in Shiva's hair.

In this drawing the artist has captured the human side of the 'Holy Family'. The depiction reveals an intimate familiarity with the characters who rest beneath a tree in an idyllic landscape of rolling hills. Shiva, shown as a naked ascetic with long, matted hair enhanced by the crescent moon, is given some drink, possibly some form of *bhang* (hemp) by Parvati. One of their sons, the six-headed Karttikeya, feeds his peacock conveyance perched on the tree while the other, the elephant-headed Ganesha, is comfortably seated before a spread of sweetmeats. Near him, Parvati's smiling lion and Shiva's dignified bull Nandi can be seen relaxing.

The 'Holy Family', drawing, Kangra, Panjab Hills, *c.* 1800

KARTTIKEYA, VALLI AND DEVASENA
ON THE PEACOCK

KARTTIKEYA IS GENERALLY referred to as the son of Shiva and Parvati. However, there are many different narratives accounting for his origin. One of the current views claims Shiva, the fire-god Agni and the river goddess Ganga all contributed to Karttikeya's origin. His name, Karttikeya 'related to the Krittikas', refers to an incident in his childhood when as a baby he was found by six goddesses, the Krittikas, who brought him up. He is one of the most mysterious and complex characters of the Hindu pantheon. Known as the god of war and the ruler of the planet Mars he is much more than the commander-in-chief of the divine armies. He is also a philosopher and a great yogi, among other things.

This god is especially popular in Tamil Nadu where he is the focus of a profoundly emotional worship. He is known as Subrahmanya 'dear to the Brahmins' or Murugan 'young man'. He is frequently depicted with one head and four arms. He sits on a throne placed on his conveyance, the peacock, a symbol of immortality. In his lower hands he carries the characteristic spear. He is flanked by his wives, the fair skinned Devasena and the dusky Valli. The trio is surrounded by a halo adorned with floral wreaths. Attendants both precede and follow the group. The peacock is shown, as is usual in southern India, with his talons firmly planted on a snake and with a snake in his beak. This is probably because the peacock is the son of Vishnu's conveyance, the eagle Garuda, a sworn enemy of the snakes.

Subrahmanya, Valli and Devasena riding on the peacock,
painting on paper, possibly from Thanjavur, *c.* 1820

GANESHA

THE OTHER SON of Shiva and Parvati is Ganesha 'Lord of the Hosts or *Ganas*' and is the most popular of the Hindu gods. As the god of wisdom, the bestower of favours, the one who helps to overcome any obstacles, he is the giver of success. Worshipped before any religious ceremony or new undertaking he is also 'Lord of the Beginnings'. If he is not duly honoured he is believed to put obstacles in one's way, hence he is also known as 'Lord of the Obstacles'.

A number of legends account for his striking appearance. One myth, in which Ganesha's parenthood is attributed to Parvati alone, narrates how Parvati fashioned a handsome youth from the dust of her body; she then took a bath and instructed her son to guard the door. Shiva, incensed at the sight of the young man who prevented his entering, decapitated the youth. Seeing Parvati's distress, he replaced the severed head with that of an elephant.

This vibrant painting shows the crowned god seated on a lotus flower. He is given a plump physique denoting well-being. In his four arms he carries an axe, an elephant goad, a rosary and a lotus flower.

Crowned Ganesha, painting on paper, Basohli, Panjab Hills, *c.* 1720

SHIVA'S BULL, NANDI

A CONVEYANCE (*vahana*) is an animal or bird associated with each Hindu god which reflects the god's personality. Perhaps the most popular among the divine conveyances is the white, humped bull Nandi whose name means 'rejoicing'. Nandi symbolizes strength, virility and fertility as well as religious and moral duties. He appears in Shaiva mythology not only as the trustworthy conveyance of Shiva but as his foremost devotee and an accomplished musician and dancer. His crouching image, often housed in a small pavilion, is at the entrance of every Shaiva temple. Nandi faces the *linga* which is enshrined in the innermost sanctuary, ready to obey to his master's summons.

Shiva's bull Nandi, granite, southern Deccan, 16th century

Devi the Great Goddess

Devi the 'goddess' is regarded as Shiva's cosmic energy and is one of the central personalities of the Hindu pantheon. Her followers worship her as the supreme entity which supports the universe. Devi has many contrasting aspects, both benevolent and fierce. Her complex, unpredictable personality is the result of a long process of assimilating local goddesses into her character. In her bountiful and nurturing aspects she is Shiva's wife Parvati 'the daughter of the mountain' and also Amba 'the mother'.

The print shows the smiling goddess Amba riding on her tiger. In her eight hands she carries a number of attributes shared also by Shiva and Vishnu. They are the discus, lotus, conch, mace and trident. This detail suggests that Amba is regarded as more powerful than Shiva and Vishnu.

Particularly interesting is the geometrical diagram in the foreground: two connected and extended triangles divided into nine compartments. The triangle symbolizes perfection, the result of unity and diversity $(1 + 2 = 3)$. Its multiple, nine, represents the ultimate perfection which is personified by Amba.

Amba 'the mother', coloured print on paper, *c.* 1973

DURGA – THE INACCESSIBLE

A FAMOUS and destructive aspect of Devi is Durga the 'inaccessible'. A long myth narrates the story of Durga which culminates in the killing of one of the god's antagonists, Mahisha the 'buffalo'.

Through steadfast meditation and rigorous penance Mahisha became all-powerful. He obtained a favour from Brahma that decreed that he could only be defeated by a woman. Engrossed in his pride, Mahisha bullied all the gods into submission and harassed them in all possible ways. The gods then decided to put an end to this situation and they assembled to meditate. Such was their power of concentration that Durga appeared in their midst as a blazing flame. As soon as she stepped out of the fire the grateful gods sung her praises and each presented her with one of their weapons. The thought of the gods being intimidated by Mahisha made her laugh, and her loud laughter made the earth tremble. This struck terror among the anti-gods and Mahisha sent his minions to see what was the cause of the earthquake. They found a beautiful, elegantly turned out, unmarried woman riding on a lion and immediately reported back to Mahisha. At the glowing description of her beauty Mahisha fell in love and sent a series of marriage proposals to her, but each offer was refused. A long battle ensued in which the best warriors of Mahisha were killed. Mahisha personally confronted the goddess and tried to defeat her by deploying his magical skills but eventually he too was defeated.

The illustration shows the climactic battle between the goddess and her antagonist. Ten-armed Durga rides proudly on her lion and transfixes Mahisha with her trident as he emerges from the decapitated buffalo carcass. This small yet powerful image was probably used for worship at home.

Durga kills Mahisha, brass and silver, possibly Mysore district,
18th-19th century

KALI – THE BLACK

THE CONFLICTS between Durga and the gods' opponents continued after Mahisha's death. During the battle the goddess became so incensed that her wrath burst out of her forehead in the form of Kali, yet another aspect of the 'Great Goddess'.

Kali 'the black' is dark, gaunt and dishevelled. She is armed with a sword, noose, skull-topped staff, her neck decorated with a garland of skulls. Kali symbolizes both the creative and destructive powers of time. Her blackness hints at the dissolution of individuality in the timeless darkness which is also filled with the potential for new life. Kali loves battlefields and cremation grounds where she dances surrounded by jackals and ghouls among the smoking funeral pyres. Sometimes, her frenzied dancing threatens the stability of the whole universe. At this point the gods plead with Shiva to intervene. He succeeds in calming her by throwing himself among the corpses under her feet.

Clay images such as this were, and still are, fashioned for the Kalipuja, one of the most important festivals in Bengal, which is cele-brated in the autumn. Once the ceremonies are completed the images are paraded through the streets and then immersed in the waters of a lake or river where they dissolve.

In Bengal artists depict Kali as a handsome woman rather than gaunt and dishevelled. Clay, Bengal, late 19th century

CHINNAMASTA – THE DECAPITATED

THE GODDESS CHINNAMASTA is probably the most explicit representation of the interdependence between sex, life and death. The awesome, decapitated goddess stands proudly brandishing a knife in one hand and triumphantly holding her severed head in the other. Three streams of blood gush from her neck: one falls in the mouth of her own severed head and the other two into the mouths of her attendants. The feet of the goddess rest on a love-making couple reclining on a lotus: Kama the god of love and, on top of him, his wife Rati, the personification of lust. Through their life-creating act they transmit vital energy into the goddess who is standing on Rati. The three streams of blood spurting from her neck show the life-energy leaving her but simultaneously feeding and sustaining her and her two attendants.

The cosmic, ever-alternating process of the giving, sustaining and taking of life is concisely but dramatically expressed here.

Chinnamasta, hand-coloured woodblock print, Bengal, 19th century

लाला शिउ रालादिन लाल   चि न्नमस्ता   छि न्नमस्तीका   कलिकाता

Vishnu

VISHNU AND CONSORTS

Among the most important Hindu deities are Shiva, Devi and Vishnu the 'all-pervasive'. Vishnu is commonly known as the preserver of the universe, he maintains the established law and order, and, most important of all, the standards of purity, a principal concern of orthodox Hindu society. When the precarious balance between good and evil is threatened Vishnu descends to earth to redress it in one of his many incarnations.

Vishnu is portrayed as a youthful and regal figure. Among his ornaments is a conspicuous sacred thread across his chest, a symbol of the higher three castes, in this case the uppermost caste, the Brahmins. His two upper hands carry the discus and the conch, and in the lower hands are the lotus and the club. Two of his attributes, the discus and to some extent the club, have become cult objects in their own right.

His two consorts are Shridevi (also called Shri Lakshmi) and Bhudevi. Shridevi personifies good fortune, beauty and prosperity. Bhudevi is the Earth goddess whom he rescues from the waters of the ocean in his incarnation as Varaha the Boar. The association of Vishnu with both goddesses reflects his royal status. In traditional Hindu thought a king is symbolically wedded to the earth and his first and foremost duty is to protect her. Shridevi is also connected with royalty because the fertility of both crops and animals and the prosperity of the population depend upon the king scrupulously following his moral duty and ritual obligations.

Vishnu with Shridevi and Bhudevi, bronze, central Tamil Nadu, *c.* 1000

GAJA LAKSHMI
'LAKSHMI WITH THE ELEPHANTS'

ORIGINALLY, LAKSHMI was a fertility goddess born from the water and connected with dung, cultivation and food. She was later associated with prosperity and became one of Vishnu's consorts.

In this painting Lakshmi's aquatic origin has not been forgotten. She sits on a lotus, emerging unsullied from the watery mud, carrying a lotus in her right hand. She wrings her wet hair with her upper pair of hands and the lower left rests on her lap. Two elephants pour water on her from the pitchers they carry in their uplifted trunks, the remaining two bathe in the lake. They have small wings, a detail which recalls a myth in which the elephants freely roamed throughout the sky. For this reason, they are associated with clouds and rain.

Gaja Lakshmi, painting on paper, Bundi, Rajasthan, *c.* 1780

VISHNU'S AVATARAS

Matsya or Fish avatara

IN MOMENTS OF CRISIS Vishnu intervenes to redress the balance between the positive and negative forces. These interventions, in which the god appears each time in a different form, are called descents (*avataras*). According to his followers, Vishnu's descents are innumerable although there are ten which are the most famous and are frequently depicted. The first incarnation, Matsya or fish, occurred when the whole creation was engulfed by water and disappeared. One of the gods' rivals snatched the four *Vedas* – the most revered scriptures of Hindu tradition – from the hands of Brahma and disappeared with them into the depths. Eventually, with Vishnu's help, they were recovered.

Vishnu is shown as half-fish and half-man carrying in his hands a discus, conch, lotus and club. Paintings such as this are typical of nineteenth-century Calcutta. They were made for pilgrims and had to be quickly produced. In order to fulfil these conditions the painters evolved a 'short-hand' style of arresting virtuosity.

Matsya *avatara*, painting on paper, Kalighat (Calcutta),
end of the 19th century

Varaha or Boar avatara

IN HIS THIRD INCARNATION Vishnu appeared as a boar to retrieve the Earth goddess, Bhudevi, from the depths of the water. Vishnu assumed the form of a gigantic boar when Hiranyaksha (one of the gods' rivals) abducted the Earth and threw her to the bottom of the sea. After a violent confrontation, at the end of which Hiranyaksha was defeated and killed by Varaha, the latter rose from the depths carrying the Earth on his tusks.

This painting shows the climax of the incident: Varaha has just slain his adversary with his formidable mace. The Earth is shown as a crescent-shaped hill with forests, gardens, mountains and streams balanced on Varaha's tusks. The artist has taken great pride in including a wealth of detail such as a temple dedicated to Shiva with a fluttering red banner while among the animals roaming the hilly landscape he has depicted a cow, a symbolic representation of the Earth goddess.

Varaha *avatara*, painting on paper, Chamba, Panjab Hills, *c.* 1740

VISHNU APPEARED as a man-lion in order to protect his great devotee Prahlada from his father, the mighty Hiranyakashipu, king of the anti-gods. The king had defeated the gods and ruled over the whole universe. He had obtained an assurance from the gods that he would not meet death at the hands of men, beasts, gods or demons, neither would he die inside or outside a house, by day or by night or by any weapon.

Hiranyakashipu had forbidden the worship of Vishnu in his kingdom. His son, Prahlada, defied his father's command and endured cruel persecutions for his unflinching devotion to the god. One day, during a conversation, the king mockingly asked Prahlada whether Vishnu, being 'all-pervading', would reside in one of the pillars of the verandah. Saying this, he kicked a pillar which burst open to reveal Vishnu as the man-lion Narasimha. He jumped out, grabbed the king and disemboweled him with his claws, all under the gaze of the awed Prahlada. Since Narasimha was not man or beast, the verandah was neither inside or outside of the house, it was not day or night but dusk, and Narasimha used his claws instead of weapons, the terms of the agreement between the king and the gods were respected.

The cult of Narasimha as an independent god still exists in remote areas of eastern Deccan and Orissa where it is believed some of the crucial events of his life took place.

Narasimha *avatara*, painting on paper, north India, early 19th century

RAMA OR RAMACHANDRA 'Rama the moon' is the seventh incarnation of the god Vishnu. His life is narrated in the *Ramayana*, an epic poem in Sanskrit, thought to be composed by the sage Valmiki. Although an incarnation of Vishnu, Rama – like Krishna – has become a deity in his own right and the focus of intense devotion.

Rama was banished from the kingdom of Ayodhya through the intrigues of the youngest of his father's wives who wanted her son to be the heir. Accompanied by his brother Lakshmana and his wife Sita he went to the forest in exile. There the three of them met with a number of adventures which culminated in the abduction of Sita by Ravana, the mighty king of Lanka. Eventually, with the help of the king of the Monkeys and the monkey-hero Hanuman, Ravana was defeated and killed. Sita was rescued but had to prove her chastity by undergoing a fire ordeal. When she emerged from the fire unscathed Rama, Sita and their followers returned to Ayodhya where Rama became king. Shortly after, Rama felt pressurized by public opinion which cast doubts on Sita's chastity after her long stay in Ravana's palace and he banished her from the kingdom. This unleashed a tragic chain of events which overshadowed the last years of his life.

Throughout his life Rama followed the path of duty: he was the dutiful son who, though unjustly banished by his father, preferred the path of exile rather than rebellion. He was an ever-attentive husband and brother and, most importantly of all, he was the model king who, by banishing Sita, put his kingly duties before his own personal happiness. Even today, Rama is celebrated as the epitome of righteousness.

Rama and Lakshmana, ivory relief, Tamil Nadu, *c.* 16th-17th century

Krishna

KRISHNA 'dark' is the eighth incarnation of Vishnu. A complex personality, Krishna is the child-god filled with mirth and mischievousness but also the slayer of a number of demons and the protector of the cowherds and their cattle. He then becomes the lover *par excellence*, a dark-skinned handsome youth playing the flute and ravishing the hearts of the local milkmaids with his appearance and haunting melodies. Later in his long career he develops into a shrewd diplomat, a great philosopher and a wise king.

Krishna is probably a pastoral deity in which the life stories of other local gods and heroes merged. Known of since the early centuries AD, Krishna became one of the most important gods of India through the pivotal influence of fifteenth and sixteenth century mystics who emphasized the emotional side of his 'biography'. Krishna's love affair with Radha, a married cowherdess, has been an inexhaustible source of inspiration for artists. Radha, the epitome of the human soul, defies social and moral conventions in order to be united with her lord.

It was Chaitanya (*c.* 1485-1533) who gave a new impetus to the Krishna cult and founded an influential philosophic school. Born in Bengal, Chaitanya moved to Puri, then travelled throughout India singing Krishna's praise and rescuing sites connected with the god's exploits from decay. Chaitanya maintained complete surrender to Krishna as the way to salvation. After his death his school was reorganized by his disciples. In 1966, A.C. Bhaktivedantaswami founded the International Society of Krishna Consciousness (ISKON) in New York which spread Chaitanya's doctrine throughout the world.

The magic of Krishna's flute, painting on paper, Mewar, Rajasthan, *c.* 1630-40

Semi-divine beings associated with Vishnu

HANUMAN

HANUMAN, whose name means 'heavy-jawed', is the monkey-hero whose fame is inextricably linked to Rama's. He is one of the most popular gods of India, famous for his prowess, selfless devotion to Rama, and for all his marvellous adventures. Gifted with superhuman powers – which are attributed to his celibacy – he can change his shape at will, a gift of great advantage in many of his exploits. His ebullient, positive and resourceful character is the perfect foil to Rama's severe, duty-conscious and, at times, remote self. Hanuman is the greatest of Rama's devotees and he is believed to sing hymns in praise of his lord when not otherwise occupied.

In this south Indian depiction he carries an uprooted tree which symbolizes his extraordinary strength. He straddles a supine warrior, probably one of Rama's enemies. Images of Hanuman are carved for protection on city gateways and fortification walls, and on slabs or boulders in remote locations.

Hanuman, brass plaque, probably Karnataka, late 18th century

GARUDA, VISHNU'S CONVEYANCE

Garuda, whose name means 'the devourer', is a mythical bird identified with an eagle or a kite. He symbolizes the wind and the all-consuming energy of the sun. Born from a huge egg, he is a hybrid creature with the legs and torso of a human and the beak, wings and talons of an eagle.

One of the central themes of Garuda's life is his continuing conflict with the snakes which began with an ancient rivalry between his mother and her sister. His mother could only be freed from bondage if Garuda would steal the nectar of immortality from heaven. Garuda flew to heaven where two formidable snakes, whose glances were deadly, guarded the nectar of immortality. Undeterred, Garuda blew dust into their eyes, stole the nectar and, after a number of other incidents, returned to earth with it and freed his mother. His exploits impressed Vishnu who granted him a favour: Garuda's request was to become Vishnu's conveyance.

Generally, the image of Garuda, kneeling respectfully with folded hands, is placed opposite the main shrine in Vaishnava temples in the same way as the crouching Nandi is placed opposite the main shrine in Shaiva temples.

Garuda, bronze, south India, *c.* 18th century

SUDARSHANA

THE ATTRIBUTES carried by the Hindu gods are, in a sense, extensions of their personalities in much the same way as their conveyances. Although most of the attributes are fleetingly mentioned in mythological works, some have a number of myths to account for their existence. One of these is Vishnu's radiant discus, Sudarshana, whose name means 'beautiful to behold'. There are various accounts of his origin. All agree in emphasizing Sudarshana's radiance, his fire-like heat and his mind-like speed. As Vishnu's attribute, Sudarshana also stands for unlimited power and swiftness in thought and action. An independent cult of Sudarshana in south India can be traced back to at least the thirteenth century.

The illustration shows him as a fierce-looking youth with side fangs in his mouth, awesome eyes and many arms which brandish weapons. Crowned with flames he emerges from a six-pointed blazing star. Sudarshana, as an independent god, symbolizes both Vishnu's infallible weapon and the impending destruction of the universe.

Sudarshana, album painting on European paper watermarked 1820, probably from Thanjavur

చక్ర త్రా శీవాశ   శ్రీ ప్యంగసుద శ కసం

FEET

INDIA HAS A LONG TRADITION of revealing the sacred through symbols: rough stones daubed with vermilion piled up beneath a tree or iron spears and metal tridents hung with garlands of marigolds are all mementoes of an all-pervasive divine presence.

Among the many symbolic depictions of a god are feet or footprints. Decorated with the appropriate symbols they represent either the Buddha, a Jaina prophet or a Hindu god. In a number of temples it is common practice to bless visitors by placing a bejewelled crown on their heads on which the divine feet or sandals are embossed.

The most famous literary reference to the symbolic significance of sandals is found in the *Ramayana* when Rama, the rightful heir to the throne, is unjustly exiled. His sandals, however, remain placed on the throne throughout the fourteen years of his absence and symbolize his presence. It is this constant rembrance of the sacred which enriches India with images of the divine.

Sacred feet, stone carving in the courtyard of the Vaidyeshvara Temple, Talakkad, Karnataka, 12-13th century

FURTHER READING

Blurton, T.R., *Hindu Art*, London, 1992 and 2001

Brockington, J.L., *The Sacred Thread: A Short History of Hinduism*, Edinburgh, 1981 and New Delhi, 1997

Dallapiccola, A.L., *Hindu Myths*, London, 2003

Eck, D., *Darsan: Seeing the Divine Image in India*, Chambersburg, 1985

Fuller, C.J., *The Camphor Flame: Popular Hinduism and Society in India*, Princeton, 1993

Huyler, S., *Meeting God: Elements of Hindu Devotion*, New Haven and London, 1999

Kinsley, D., *Hindu Goddesses: Visions of the Divine Feminine on the Hindu Religious Tradition*, Berkeley and New Delhi, 1986

Michell, G., *The Hindu Temple: An Introduction to its Meaning and Forms*, London, 1977

Michell, G., ed., *Temple Towns of Tamil Nadu*, Bombay, 1993

O'Flaherty, W.D., *Hindu Myths: A Sourcebook Translated from the Sanskrit*, Harmondsworth, 1975

Zimmer, H., *Myths and Symbols in Indian Art and Civilization*, Princeton, 1972

ILLUSTRATION REFERENCES

Page

2 Photograph by A.L. Dallapiccola

6 Cambridge-Kumbakonam Project

11 Photograph by A.L. Dallapiccola

13 BM, OA 1974.4-17.014

15 BM, OA 1910.11-7.3

17 BM, OA 1948.10-9.0156

19 BM, OA 1993.7-24.02

21 Photograph by A.L. Dallapiccola

23 Arcaid Picture Library

25 Photograph by A.L. Dallapiccola

27 BM, OA 1959-4-11.07

29 BM, OA 1990-10-20-07

31 Photograph by A.L. Dallapiccola

33 Photograph by A.L. Dallapiccola

35 BM, OA 1880-304

37 Cambridge-Kumbakonam Project

39 Photograph by A.L Dallapiccola

41 Photograph C Branfoot

43 Photograph by A.L. Dallapiccola

45 Photograph by A.L. Dallapiccola

47 Photograph by A.L. Dallapiccola

49 Photograph by A.L. Dallapiccola

51 BM, OA 2001 11-26.1

53 BM, OA 1966-10-14-1

55 Photograph by A.L. Dallapiccola

57 BM, OA 1969, 12-16, 1

59 BM, OA 1939, 3-11, 02

61 BM, OA 1974, 6-7.014 (7)

63 BM, OA 1966.2-12.03

65 BM, OA 1923.3-6.1

67 Photograph by A.L. Dallapiccola

69 BM, OA 1919.11-4.40

71 BM, OA 94.2-16.10

73 BM, OA 1993.10-8.02

75 BM, OA 1965.10-17.3, 4

77 BM, OA 1956, 7-14, 032

79 BM, OA 1949.0409.85

81 BM, OA 1966.7-25.01

83 BM, OA 1880. 2063

85 BM, OA 1995.10.6.1

87 BM, OA 1959.4-11.07

89 BM, OA 1853 1-8-8

91 BM, OA 1995 4-3.1

93 BM, OA 1962 12-31.01 (12)

95 Photograph by A.L. Dallapiccola